THE LAY OF
ELEANOR AND IRENE

The Lay of
Eleanor and Irene

Brooks Haxton

The Countryman Press
Woodstock, Vermont

A portion of this work first appeared in the Spring, 1983 issue of *The Kenyon Review*.
This edition is published in 1985 by The Countryman Press, Woodstock, Vermont 05091.

Library of Congress Cataloging in Publication Data

Haxton, Brooks, 1950-
   The lay of Eleanor and Irene.

   I. Title.
PS3558.A825L3   1985   811'.54   85-6717
ISBN 0-88150-039-9 (pbk.)

for Francie
sine qua non

ACKNOWLEDGMENTS

I would like to thank Syracuse University for supporting me with a University Fellowship while I finished and revised this poem. I would also like to acknowledge the help of George Elliott, who, despite countless other demands on his time, read a large part of the poem in manuscript and offered his characteristically clear, unhedged, and useful comments. Philip Booth and Hayden Carruth have supported me in this and other work not only with friendship and with serious attention and painstaking editorial advice, but by the powerful example of their writings and dedicated service in the community of artists. Andy Robbins has helped by lending an ear and expressing a poet's enthusiasm while the poem was in progress and by sharing his keen critical intelligence while I was reworking the unfinished whole. Conversations with Harris McCarter helped me to articulate the animating insights of the poem. By publishing the first part of this poem in the *Kenyon Review* and by sharing his generous creative energies, Frederick Turner has been an indispensible support. Thanks to my brothers and friends for lifting my spirits with their warm attention. My parents have fostered my writing with their love, and have shared their expertise and wisdom as artists and as readers and livers of lives — for all that, which is beyond description, thanks.

The Lay of
Eleanor and Irene

ONE

One reason I was following her
Into the Red Apple
At Broadway and 88th was
That on West 93rd
From the upheld swordtip
Of the statue of Jeanne d'Arc
The sun at solstice had been pouring
Red light like red wine
Over her white cotton skirt
And into that translucent
Chalice between her legs.

I fell witness to the event
In a spirit not foreign to that
Of the scientists in Principe
Who photographed the apparent
Dislocation of stars
Near the sun's limb during
Eclipse. Their evidence, they claimed,
Proved: gravity bends light—
Which Einstein already knew.

My thoughts, if not foreign to theirs,
Were neither quite the same,
When I looked at that incandescent
Shape between dancer's legs—
Equations having been proven
Adequate, in one case,
To incredible facts,
And Imagination again
Borne out in the stars; while,
In the case of the sunset,
The dancer, and myself—
A less celestial congress, or
Syzygy more mundane—

3

The apparent dislocation disturbed
Not the stars but me, and
No scientific law
Appeared to apply, because
While I followed the dancer
Between walls of available goods
An equally handsome woman,
Whom I loved, was expecting me home.

The sexual urge in man
Is psychosomatic. That means,
However often you hear
That story about stampede
(The corpuscle herd hellbent
Barging through Bottleneck Gap
Into Box Canyon where,
Unable to budge, they low
And wag a belligerent horn),
However often you hear that
The genie inside the lamp
Applied his potent craft
Without Aladdin's consent,
You may still tend to suspect
The more or less controlled
Suppression of pertinent fact—
For instance: having slipped wine jars
Over the lead steer's horns,
The cowpokes were trying to see
Who could shoot them off,
When, for reasons at that time abstruse,
The stampede must have commenced.

Mine was a typical case:
An unregenerate urge
To tipple the faint blush of light
Between strenuous thighs,
To cup knees in one's palms
And feel them drift apart.

4

If seduction presupposes
Having seduced oneself,
I was not unseduced at heart:
I felt that the dancer must
Be averting her passion for me
Toward the selection of fruit,
As, in the *Kama Sutra*,
A courtesan at first
Provokes the imagination
By showing her intimacy with
An animal or a child.

The green mango she picked by
Cupping it to her face
And inhaling the southerly fume
Suggested a communion other
Than tête à tête over dessert;
Ancient ecstatic rites
In an equatorial dark,
Small undergrowth concealing
The cleft lip of a spring
Where luxurious orchids bloomed.

On uncharted waters
Between the Island of Venus
And her Estate in the brain,
I felt a swoon cast anchor;
The boat listed after the racket
Of whipped out lengths of chain;
And the notion of things below—
Swift, however prolonged,
Like the dream of an unending fall,
At the lower margin of light,
Like a forsaken thought,
Confoundingly incomplete
And urgent for resolution
As a symphonic phrase—

The notion of things below now
Having anchored the discourse above,
I could begin my approach
To the actual body at hand by

Asking her, "How can you tell
When a mango's green if it's ripe?"

Where she had seen me before—
That her one questioning look,
On a molecular level
Coupling broken connections
And changing the baths of nerves,
Lighted Mnemosyne's lamp
Faintly, far back, in one eye—
I was afraid to know.

As Venus Anadyomene
Crossing the foam at dusk
Flickers out when you look
But beams when you look aside,
She tilted her chin and said,
"Aren't you Eleanor's friend?"
By which she meant not friend
But father held over as son,
Bane of her being, her beau,
The windfall of her wandering eye,
Her cocksman, her keeper, her catch.

"Oh. Yeah. We live up the street.
I thought you lived in Soho,"
I said not to contest
The fact that she lived where she lived,
But to foster any impression
That I might know who she was,
To steal from her for the succuba
Whom I had followed here
An illusion of bodily warmth,

But the succuba had withdrawn,
The mojo withdrew from the mango,
And I was alone in the aisle,
Not that the mango wasn't
Nesting still in my palm
While I held it forth to the dancer
Nonchalantly as though
I were king of the gypsies
And it, a crystal ball,
Only the mango minus
The *Kama Sutra* karma
That made my pose apropos
Seemed to have trebled its weight,
For here I was with a stranger
In a subtemperate city
Handling tropical fruit.

Boreas poured from the shelves
Of the frozen food section behind me.
All around me lay
A commercial version of nature
Keeping nature at bay—
Seedpods of metallic foil,
Garish peels of paper,
Cardboard husks, glass eggshells,
Wombs and udders of clear plastic,
Stores that the elements
In harness had already
Pickled, salted, boiled, dried,
Smoked, baked, and frozen
For those copy writers call
Smart shoppers, while, abroad,
Others, dumb with hunger,
Died; but not I nor the dancer.

We stood still in the aisle
Considering how best to reconnoiter.

"You weren't with Eric at the seafood
Dinner Dale gave in his loft
Last fall," I asked, managing
To make that fact sound not
Remotely like a question.

Her eyes, I saw then, were gray blue,
The cast of woodsmoke raveling
Into the cobalt of unclouded sky.
The iris of the right contained
Three drops of jade
Under the pupil, and the left,
A splintered thread of green-
Glanced-through-with-gold. That I'd
Not seen these eyes in Dale's
Or anybody's loft,
Not ever, anywhere
Before, I had no doubt now,
For my pupils and her pupils met.

When the delusion that sight
Penetrates the seen
Has come dislodged, creation,
Opening the floodgates of the eyes,
Pours back into itself,
Till "understanding" describes
Not the drilling rig
But an artesian well
Where Thirst repairs at nightfall
To draw streams of thought,
As I at the anomaly
Of the dancer's eyes.

Now, though, epistemology
Seemed least of my concerns.
The question of the siren song
Perplexed me more.

　　　　　　While
Down Broadway prowl cars tore
With sirens blaring, the quintuple
Sirens of the senses
To the mind's Odysseus
Unmercifully sang.

If sirens in Greek waters lay
Without the mariner's reach,
They never were on that count
Less alluring or less real:

To *hear* therefore across
The navigable gulf
Of only an arm's length of air
The song of what she said;
To *see* the matrix of her eye;
To *sniff* (under the mask
Of onions wizening)
The herbs in her shampoo;
And to anticipate the *touch*
And *taste* of that taut flesh
Over the tendon in her neck—
Though I should never nip
Nor suckle there while throbs
Tugged in my lights and chills
Splashed the ripplings of my back,
Yet—: the awareness of her
Was what would have been
An urge, but what felt now not,
As an urge, original in me,
But like the siren song
Apart and other, absolute,
In sway, and ineluctable.

With her the operations
Of the will worked as they might
On the desire to breathe
Deep underwater
Where thoughts tease and escape
And no one finds words to regret
The invitation—every nerve
Upon the blood's insistence
Sends one—to inhale.

She said, "No. I don't think
We've met. I recognize you
From the picture. How
Is Eleanor? She must
Have told you about me.
I'm Irene?"

       "Oh. Irene."

TWO

If Eleanor had ever mentioned
Irene, I had missed
Not merely what she said,
But nuances that might have told me
How much I was choosing
Not to know.

           I said,
"Yes. Eleanor's told me
About you. It's too bad we haven't
Had the chance to meet."

Irene glanced from the mango
I was holding to the one
She held still with both hands
Snug to her pubic bone,
And under the cosmetic blush
Blood rose kindling in her cheeks.

What that blush meant—or the shrug
That turned up in one hand
Her mango, ripe and green—
I could not have begun to tell.

The power I lacked, and longed for,
Was an animal's good sense
To read her ambiguities
In lieu of words, by scent,
By the composure of the limbs,
By the dilation of blood vessels
In the cheeks, by faith
In an unreasoning attention
To the just perceptible
Transmissions of the eyes.

Failing that, I fell back
On habitual misunderstandings.
I conceived a problem of intent
Where reason and desire described
Axes in Descartes' plane,
Relative to which Irene and I,
At any single moment,
Drew two vectors oriented
More or less toward bed.

Holding her fruit forth to me
As I had held forth mine
To her, looking as much
Misgiven as amused,
Irene, voice trembling, said,
 "Well, the way you know,
When mangos are ripe? is
The way they feel and smell.
They get this sharp, sweet,
Musty kind of smell,
And they should be firm but not hard
Like, uh, like . . ."

                    "An avocado?"

"Yes, like an avocado."

The brotherhood of five,
Gone underground, conspired
At crossroads, changing signs,
To lose intelligence
In the familiar landscape
Of the flesh, to leave me
Like an acrobat mid-flip,
Blindfolded, between wobbling bars,
While, in a mounting fugal
Counterpoint, my thoughts
Rehearsed rococo variations
On the text of "Baby, me and thee."

To stanch the wound in that four-handed
Golden forebear of iron
Lovelorn Aristophanes—
That is, to scourge the mind
Of a millenia-dividing thought—
I thought that I could come
To Irene not the yearning halved
Hyperborean but whole,
Individual, and free.

"I don't know. The truth is . . ."
I began, intending to confide
That Eleanor had told me nothing
Memorable about anybody
Named Irene, but got cut off.

Irene—disarmed, I thought,
By my libido basso which,
Under a contralto strain
Of pure remorse, kept warbling
De profundis a brass callnote—
Gasped, like the bassoonist for a solo,
And broke in with, "Why don't we
Go talk at my place? It's not far."

Not to reveal my
Turbulent delight and fright,
I nodded my head frowning.
"I need to pick up a few things.
I'll meet you by the register."

Having got the invitation
That I had expected—
Only after many
Trial humiliations—
Finally to be denied,
I found myself not happy,

Not relieved, but subject
To the spells of storm and calm
That sweep mind over body
As a hurricane sweeps ocean
Over island and recedes.

The shoreline returns drenched, blanketed
With shards, with swatches torn
From boats, from piers, from houses,
Strewn with navigation markers,
Nets and cyclone fences,
Whole trees—limb, leaf, root-system—
Plucked up and dropped, like dandelions,
And the harbor town, the coastal
Wilderness, bear crush marks
Where, at random, coupling
Fall and summer winds pitched
In enormous, giddy throes.

The things I'd said I needed
To pick up I couldn't find.
In household wares, aisle two,
I tried to pick up the lost thread
Of eight years' thought
Concerning Eleanor,
My never-yet- but maybe soon-
To-be-betrayed near-wife,
With whom I had made homes
In two empires, one failed
And one still failing: Rome
The former, and here now New York.

First, Rome: she-wolf, implacable,
In bronze, astride the twins
Bernini, after ninety
Generations, foisted
At her swollen teats,

As though the city, and the nurture
Of the murderous, began
When savage nature suckled
Perfect cherubim,
And not when childhood thoughts
Divided thee from me
And us in common from all kind.

Rome, where virgin woods
Fell for the settlements
That prosperous Etruscans
Made a town, whose craftsmen
Worked in pigments and baked earth
To celebrate their patrons'
Singular delight
In funerals with flutists,
Dancing, flowers, drink,
And food, before their patrons
And their patrons' retinues,
Their goods, and all they knew,
Were by commotion of barbarians
Erased, while what had been
Their country town became
Most warlike, wealthiest,
Most feared of cities, and remained
A good millenium until
Its law, and certain walls,
Gave way, and tides of refuse
Rose, and rubble, and raw earth,
First in the tenements, and soon
Inside the senate and the temple,
In the marketplace, around
Tall obelisks and figures
Winding in procession
Up commemorative columns,
Up, to swamp the portals
Of triumphal arches where
Homecoming indomitable armies
Had been wont to strut, decked
In the panoply of the victorious.

15

There, in the piazza
Where we lived, palms grew,
And early mornings the deserted
Marketplace unfolded
Bare stands more abundant
Than a blossoming limb's length of buds,
Till all the neighborhood
Of women swarmed about
In their dark clothes to fill
Expandable net bags with cheese
And eggs and vegetables,
With fruit and fish and flesh,
With hens with unplucked heads,
And daily bread.

                    But noon
Toppled into midnight between stands
Folded into caskets while
Beside the empty street
Whores under streetlights watched
For men: whom shoppers there
That morning had gone home
To feed; whose lackluster
Fucking followed in full view.

Has what I've understood
Least well most often been
What I've become? If not,
Is there no point in its still
Seeming so?—I wondered,
While I watched Irene
Cross at the far end of aisle two.
                              *
If Eleanor and I made
Love less year by year,
We had at least kept faithful,
I maintained. In Rome, though,
We'd made love as the Etruscans
Banqueted. We basked

16

In an auroral flush
That hardly faded when we quit
To sleep. We bathed in time,
In swirling hours drawn
From an unstinting source
None witnesses to spill
Into the dark few can remember,
And that few, amiss, though not
For long. We mourned with moans
And infant cries the deaths
In childbed of all ecstasies,
But, as the Etruscans did,
We made of mourning, by
Strict observation, ceremonies
Of delight, in which the pang
Of loss accedes to praise.

What changed? How much! That I,
Lips parted, could be mumbling,
Fondling the cool hourglasses
Of the Wesson Oil,
While Irene's supple buttocks,
In aisle three, flexing and relaxing
With her walk, appeared more glorious
Than the election into paradise,
And memories of my love knot
Seemed impertinent
As an addendum on the failings
Of a disillusioned empire.

Time now to meet Irene,
Nothing but mango in hand.
Near the detergents I felt
Soap at the back ledge
Of my tongue leak down my craw
And in the vinegar's vicinity
An acrid fume lift
Through my sinuses.
The Sentimental Strings

On Muzak overhead
With an insipid dip tripped
My seasickness mechanism.
An insurgent body walked
Aisle two in that remove
Where one's own legs assume
Autonomy disquieting
As the aplomb of centipedes.

"You get all you need?"
Inquired Irene.

                "No,
I needed some green chilies,"
I said, inconsolably,
With an averted look
That found in her two hands
Still nothing but her mango.

Then, I smiled.

THREE

On Broadway night had begun
Veiling the electric eyes
Of streetlights under salmon-tinted
Streaks of mackerel sky.
The sun behind the Palisades
West on 88th showed
No more brilliant, though more saturated
Red, than an ascendant, half
Augmented moon over
My shoulder east. The Belnord
Stood in the planet's shadow.

At the corner I said, "Have
You lived in the neighborhood long,
Irene?"

        She pressed my forearm
With her fingertips lightly,
As she would an open door,
To close the opening but not
The latch, as though to tell
A secret, but she did not speak.

We walked the block to West End
Without talking, while the sun's
Bright Japanese decal
Slid into an imperial
Blue envelope of clouds.

Transvestites who'd been lounging
On the hoods of cars retired
Into the mirrored hall
Of Central Apt. Hotel.

At West End I looked north
And south and saw, east
Of the avenue pitched
Over little hills, striations
Of apartment buildings lapped
By bands of masonry
And hatched with evanescent
Rings and films of light.

Transcendence and shortwindedness caught
At my heart.

My thoughts cleared:

Home, where Eleanor sat
Knitting on the couch,
I laid hands, foreign to me
For their having touched the breast
And belly and the lower lip
Of Irene, foreign as they were,
I laid these hands on the familiar
Neck of Eleanor, and smiled
And kissed her mouth, and knew
What she could not know, though she asked,
"Where have you been out so late?"

The light changed and we crossed West End.

The first trees we walked past
Were sycamores in which
Crepuscular phantasms
Of faint light and wind
Quietly ransacked the leaves.

Irene paused at the bottom step
Of the first stoop, blurted,
"This is it," and darted up.

The furrow of her naked back,
Sciaticus to cervix,
Undulated in the black
V of the leotard
Between swinging arms.
Bare calves, large from their tilting
Of the slippered heels,
Bulged on full application
Of the toes into the spring
Of each ascending step.

I stood immobile under her,
Under a thousand fans
Of gingko leaves, and thought,
"Not possible! So perfect
In its architecture! To be mine!"

Opening the door, she turned,
And I began, halfheartedly,
To mount the irreversible
Ascent toward incognita
As though it were nothing more
Than a front stoop.

        Inside
The dark hall, in the cool,
Images of two bodies swam
Under the surface of a more-
Than-full-length mirror on the right.
We swam between the still glass
And the stained oak for no more
Than one breath's duration.
No more than seven heart
Beats' breadth, we swam. She,
In composure as accomplished
As the leader of a promenade,
I, tripper over throw rugs
With apologies to the floor,

Sponsor of distress, receding
Shocks of early gray,
Disheveled, deep lines under eyes
Downcast, swam into
And across the objectivity,
The absolute disinterest,
And relentless clarity
Of this illusion, and stepped
Onto the far shore at the foot
Of a steep flight of stairs.

I found myself in the lacuna
Of epistemologies, between
The chemical and electric works
Of the receptive organs
And an office where the memory
Construes from its labsheets
And fading, partial registers
Expedient, however plausible, truths.

At some such pass, between
The evident and my
Propensity to know,
I found myself, not simply
Ignorant, but like
That transitory impulse
On the optic nerve,
At once unknowing and sole character
Of what was to be known.

I climbed the stairs three steps
Behind Irene, eyes true
To the orbital motion of her ass.
Under my breastbone dismay
Rampaged against my heart.
My breath came short. My lungs
Kept begging to be filled.
Slight fibrillations rippled
Me to the quick. I gasped.

"Just one more flight," she said,
And bounded up.

                    And why
Was Irene bringing me home?
I had assumed to fuck,
But her laconic, not
To say occult, demeanor
Was portending weird
Waystations, while I fidgeted
To keep panic, less and less
Strategically, in check.

Unseen, around the corner,
Overhead, keys
Glided into keyholes,
Tumblers tumbled, bolts
Scraped from their sockets,
And the bar of her police lock
Rode the ringing clangor
Of its groove. An orgy
Of unfastening rattled
The involuntary ear.

Irene stood facing me
Across the closing crack
Of her apartment door

Shut. Then, sounds again, of metal,
Then feet moving.

                    I,
Lightheaded from the climb,
Veered left across the landing
Toward her, toward where nothing
But the number 3
Of brass would stay in focus.

Graces and weird sisters,
Unbefriending heads of Cerberus,
The earth and sun and moon,
And birth and life and death,
The grammar book's three persons,
She and you and I,
Vestiges of creatures
Cast in any of three pairs,
Male, and female, mated,
Love, in the lien of hate,
Squandering three wishes
Or three guesses or three tries:
Fascinations of the number three
Did not fascinate me now.

The fastness of the door
Between me and Irene did.

FOUR

I posed the problem first
As a review in protocol.

(1) Shall a caller, having
Been invited and summarily
Locked out, presume to knock
Or
(2)   Does eleventh hour
Locking out, in etiquette,
Gainsay an invitation?

(3) If this question stands in doubt,
Does tact or dignity
Permit the supplicant
To sue for his admittance
With mute station at the door
Or
(4)   Self-esteem require
Uncompromising, if not quite
Felicitous, retreat?

Of these four alternatives
The odds, neither in the least
More tenable than its even
Opposite, still took
The first eliminations.

Now, whether to demand
As would befit a father
Of a daughter, with insistent
Reasonable knock, or to entreat,
As has befallen sons
Of mothers, with a silent,
All-deserving look,
Remained in doubt; not, mind you,
That my thinking followed any
Such syntactical discourse.

It flowed, my thinking, flowed
Into the mind, through time,
Took time to make a path,
A waterway that wound
Out of the future's cloud
And mountainside to spill
Abruptly at this ledge
Into an oceanic,
Worry-making past.

It flowed the other way
Too, from coverts of completion
Through the open country here
Toward where no shore is visible.

Both ways at once it went,
In retrograde and on,
Time-altering, like a fugue
Or like the luminous
Spattering on the walls
Of what we claim to know
By naming it the universe,
The stars that dive toward earth
And into nothingness
At once, at speeds beyond which
Things, according to reliable
Equations, cease to be.

Should words or numbers or
Nine-billion-year-old waves
Of light appear to tell
A story, people say,
"It's true," by which they mean
Not inconceivable, or
"False," meaning inconvenient.
Faith, fatuous enough,
Comprises knowledge.

I

Did not know what to do
Because my faith in protocol
Was insecure. I tried
Recurring to emotions.
Fear was predominant.
Fear what Irene's tale
To Eleanor's friends might be.

"I met Eleanor's lover.
He'd been following me.
I tried to be polite,
You know, invited him up.
But he kept giving me such a
Hungry look, I got the creeps
And locked him out of my apartment.
I hope it didn't hurt
His feelings. For a while
He stood around outside the door
Like some kind of zombie."

I knocked twice
            Twice
                        And again.

"I'm sorry. Isn't it open?"
Irene's voice came through the muffling
Oak slab and sheet metal door
Locked three times by her.

I could hear behind me
Pairs of shadows tiptoe
Into the slit of light
Under the door opposite
Irene's, number 6. An eye
Of indeterminate gender
Stopped the effluence
Of lamplight through the peephole.
"It is a man."

                    "Move over."

"Let me see."

                    "Who is it?"

"Won't she let him in?"

"It is a man."

                    "Hush. Now, move.
I still haven't seen. Why,
It is a man."

                    Three anile
Whispers, low but loud enough
To reach the deaf-with-age
And me, corroborated
One another's and my own
View that "it is a man."
This postulation, crucial
As it clearly was,
Did not perplex me then
As much as number 6's
Being made to face 3
In a house with only two
Apartments on each floor.

Irene was opening her door.
"I'm sorry. Living alone,
You know, a woman, locks
Are automatic, I mean,
You know, coming home.
You just can't wait sometimes.
It's good to have a door
This solid, I don't mean
For you, but on the street

It's dangerous. I don't know.
I can't breathe till I get
These locks turned. The front door's
Like nothing. I am sorry.
It's a reflex. You know?"

"Uh huh. What about the weirdos
In apartment six.
Don't they guard the place?"

"Shh! One of them can hear,"
She said, locking the door
After us with all three locks.

"They're nice ladies, really,
Once they get you inside
Their apartment. They're
Just funny about letting
Anybody in.
Even after they get
To know you, they'll still fight
About whose turn it is
To give you the once-over
Out front at the peephole.
Inside, though, they're nice.
They used to be ballerinas.
Now that they're landladies
They rent mainly to ballerinas."

"This is their house?"

                    "That's right."

"And they live all in one room?"

"Yes. Well, I didn't say
They're not eccentric."

29

               "Why
Is number six across
The hall from number three?"

From Irene's half-step backwards
From the slump of her square shoulders,
From the vacant groping
Of her lips to close,
I gathered that my trivial question,
Meant to keep this talk
Uncontroversial, failed.

Her eyes broke, not away
But through, toward an unbreachable
Recess of thought. The droplets
Under the right pupil,
Globular as apples
Of Hippomenes,
Held me back, while she
Withdrew over the alpha wave,
Straining to right herself
Painstakingly.

              Her shoulders
Reared in arcs, and down
Her backbone slow waves
Of articulation drew
The sunken ribcage forth
While she took one deep breath.
Her breasts, uprising, shone
Like smallish moons under
The dusky leotard,
So clear, I thought I saw
The flood flush through the aureole
While her right nipple grew
Erect.

At this, my blood,
More radical than the Atlantic
At the Bay of Fundy,
Poured its tide in homage
Into a member shrunk
With fear.

The fear struck deeper
While my erection doubled,
Snagged by the glans penis
On the crotch seam, wherefrom
It sprang broadside, stopped
With audible, immodest
Whack by the cool flank
Of the inner thigh.

I blushed.

Irene, her resolute
Yet vulnerable splendid eyes
Still fixed on something not me
But in my locale, said,
"OK. Let's talk straight.
Wait a minute," and left
The room,

That is, me,
Four chairs, a table, bookshelves,
Walls chalk white and bare,
Thirteen-foot ceiling,
Kitchen alcove under
Loft bed to which
Half a wooden stepladder
Was tacked with forty-penny
Nails: a studio, then,
One huge, almost empty
Room Irene left
Through the kitchen for the john.

I trailed my forefinger
The length of one bare wall
Until, at bay in the bay
Window, I saw: darkening
Facades of brownstones, some
With tenants busy in bright rooms;
The speckled stub of one
New Jersey highrise, backlit
By the decrescendo
Of refracted long wavelengths of light;
And the pedestrians and traffic
Down on 88th: a world
Surrounded by the mind
As water by the tongue,
As wilderness by one's campfire,
While at my side in air
The tip of my forefinger
Tingled, as though touching
With its local memory
The surface of the wall.

My penis had shrunk back to nothing
By the time Irene
Stepped onto the dance floor,
Her walk, a manifesto —
The compliance of leg muscle,
The implacability of back,
The poise of a curved hand
Borne with plasticity
And self-possession of elbow
And wrist — movements drafting
Such emphatic charters
On the emptiness
They crossed, the scene became
For me a déjà vu.

I told her, "I could swear
I stood here and you came

32

Across like that sometime
Before. Way back sometime.
You ever get that feeling?"

"No." Speech uninflected
As her walk was mindful.
"You don't have to do this.
I said I would talk straight."

I didn't think she meant
In such flat tones to set
The mood for anything
Like "Do you wanna fuck?"
But nothing else I had
In mind seemed honest enough
To bring up. "OK . . . uh . . . uh . . ."

Irene began, half as though
Explaining to herself,
"It's up to Eleanor. I mean,
Why talk to me? Isn't it
Between you and her?"

"I guess." I couldn't guess,
Though, what was between
Me and anybody. I'd gotten
Queasier.

            Having butterflies makes
Ulcer victims like me chrysalises
For imagos outfitted
With hook and harrow to tear free.

    What's born is pitiful,
    The butterfly, obese,
    With tiny crushed fans pumping
    And uncrumpling from its bloated body.

    Four minutes pass.

             Fluid
From the body's reservoir
Subsides into the wings.

A narrow beauty now,
Illuminated to the quick,
With native brilliance as
An aviatrix, dares
Unaccommodating weather,

Skims treetops,

                    Disappears.

Irene took stock of the pain
Registered by my squint.
She kept time in her step,
Bay window to bare table,
Crossing the inflections
Of her footfall with her speech,
"You can't expect *me* to stop
Seeing *her*. If that's why
You *followed* me, don't ask."

"O." Eleanor was . . . Irene
Was . . . They . . .

FIVE

Even before
I could manage jealousy
Came an involuntary
Impulse to console Irene.

I was supposed to feel heartbroken—
I knew that—and angry, well,
OUTRAGED! APPALLED! Why would *I*
Want to console anyone?

Hadn't I been cuckolded,
Made light of, hell! replaced!
By her with her airy walk?
And *that*, that vulnerable
Female spirit, hurt now,
Drooping, wasn't it the very
Instrument of the betrayal?
And should *I* console *her*?

And why not?

When here she stood,
Groping an empty chair,
Rocking it to sleep,
Lullabying *it*, poor thing,
Already having waked herself
Past recourse into the nightmare
Of her choosing.

Of my choosing.

Ours. A mutual nightmare.
For hadn't I chosen to allow
The rift between us, between
Eleanor and me, the rift

So tiny as to be mere
Probability, hardly
Enough to be considered,
Hadn't I chosen to stand by
And watch that rift come open?

Not on purpose. After all,
Who'd argue purpose?
So immaculate were hazard,
History—you name it.

But how could I? Have
Consoled her I mean.

                            When
She didn't turn, and now
Her voice, accelerando,
Went crescendo, quavering,
"Why come here then? Why torment me?
I don't come around
To torment you. You, you were
The lucky one. You lived
With her and didn't even
Have to know about me. I
Have had to know about you
From the beginning. Can't you
Just go away?"

                            If she
Had known since 93rd
That I'd been following her,
Why, rather than escaping
Home, had she gone shopping?
For the mango? For me? Could
This revelation have been planned?

"I will go now if you're
Not ready. I just think

It would be good for us
To talk." *She'd better talk,*
The bitch!

            The backsurge
Of her breathing broke
On an inaudible sob.

Did she mean to leave me
Like this? Have me go home
Now? I had pretended
I knew what was happening
In the Red Apple, hadn't I?

And what did I know now?
Nothing—but that I was lost.

I lusted for Irene but
Eleanor's was whose hair
Was in my clothes, whose meltings
Tasted on my tongue,
Whose language came like smoke
Out of my mouth, was she
Of me, was I, was who
Was giving head with Irene who

Said, "I don't mean to be this way.
I'll make some tea. Sit down."

Behind me and on both sides
Were dark windows; here, before me
Glaringly white walls,
A sleeping chair, two mangos
On an otherwise bare table,
And Irene.

Can the whole
World fly to pieces—scatter
Like a pocketwatch dropped
On a dark flight of stairs?

The chair moaned in its sleep
When I sat down. Instead
Of trying to make sense
Of me—or Eleanor—and Irene,
I took the mangos in my palms
And pondered one against the other
As though they were the choices
To be made.

                    "You want one
Of these with tea?"

                    "Why not?"

"Where can I find a fruit knife
And a bowl?"

                    "I've only got
One kitchen knife." She handed me,
Blade toward herself, a butcher
Knife well over a foot long.

Having let her put the handle
To my palm, I closed my hand
And kept examining the blade:
The ragged edge; the tip—
Where she had wanted to pry
Something loose—broken,
Then, wrenched widdershins
By failure, maybe, to remove
A screw; where handle met
Blade tarnished but still
Mirrorlike enough that

I could see in splotches
Its peculiar version of
Myself, the broad face of
Dementia, of an oaf
Or angel of the Early
German School, an apparition
Unaccountably serene
In the observance of
The offertory blade.

"A bowl and a plate for the peels."
She set them on the table.

I'd been brought here on *my*
Pretext, though she never did
Confirm it, so that I
Would have to make believe
I'd known. Or look a fool.
Only I looked a fool
Making believe, because
Irene had given me no choice.
She'd given me: a motive
And the knife.

        A scruple lodged
Between left eye and brain.
A tiny muscle in the eyelid
Twitched while I stared down
The angel in the blade.

Why not stab the woman?
I could ask, I thought,
Since I knew better
Than to try, but asking
Gratified me so much
That I tried suggesting it.

You could stab the bitch. You know?

Something thrilled at different
Phrasings of it. Not
That it was faintly possible.
It had occurred to me,
However, when my palm
Began to sweat, that on
Impact one's grip could slide,
One's fingers get cut, and
Then Eleanor would know.

Is talking nonsense to
Oneself premeditation?
Not if you're not planning
Anything. Besides,
How would the jury find out?

Did thinking these things make
Me a psychopath?

Who knows when fantasy
Will flood the mesh of organs
Into an actual
Address? If they could tell,
Why would the specialists
Be prone to suicide?

Item: right hand damp,
Unsteady; knuckles flushed
In declivities.

Victim:
Who was to be the victim?

Irene, off at the periphery
Of my vision, spooned Oolong
Into the pot and noted
The dilemma not at all.

Though the butcher-blade might
Wobble; apparition flutter;
Intellect misdoubt
The title to the engines
Of the hand, the mind:
How should there be a victim?

Irene when she turned saw
No sign of an angel except me,
My stupefaction planted
In the trance the chair was in,
Trickling from my slack mouth
An elastic strand of drool.

Who was to be the victim?

I, who made the feeble
Snap now after the drop
That landed on the table?

And said, "Fuck am I in sad shape!"

"Yes."

     No! There was to be
No victim. There was to be
Only the sorry lot
Of us, at which I laughed
Until tears started and
I cried—tears from the time
When Eleanor and I
Began to make ourselves
Unhappier than we could say—
Tears, however ignorant,
Of joy, because I need not
Lose my wits or hurt Irene
But could succumb to tears,

Now that they wet my lips,
Of weakness, and inside my mouth
The savor of humiliation,
The defeat, and anger at betrayal,
The enormousness of being
In a white room west
Of West End after dark.

SIX

She had begun to cry
Too by the time I could
Accept the cup of tea.

The prominences of her skull —
The cheekbone, brow, and jaw
At angles in the clouded
Flesh where freckles drank
Raw umber from blue sources
Underneath — grew less
Acute the more the lips
And eyelids thickened while she cried.

She caught me watching her,
And, kind as it made her look
To cry, now that she laughed,
Looked even kinder;

And she looked through tears,
Through steam, through tears again,
Into the fundus of the eye,
Through her reflection on the dome,
Into her likeness in the basin,
Into the sparks and fluid,
Into the subterranean current,
Where, in the faintest likelihood
Of any being there to tag
"The culprit," she saw me.

I could feel my being seen,
And I saw from far back,
Out of the browbone's shadow,
Over the precipice of the cheek,
Saw someone, intimate
And unfamiliar, smile,

Embarrassed to have cried
And to have seen me cry,
But unapologetic
And unasking of apologies,
For no one wants to ask,
Or to be asked by,
Nemesis for a break.

She lifted her cup to snap
The binding of our looks,
Lifted it in both hands,
The way she had lifted
The mango; closing her eyes,
Inhaled; and, opening them, said,
"You want me to slice that now?"

What sane reason could one have
For saying no?

         "I don't care
For any, thanks."

         "Did Eleanor
Know you wanted to talk
With me?"

         "I don't think
She knows I've found out yet."

"How long have you known?"
Peeling the mango made
Her hands look slender,
Womanly, all-competent.
I wanted to surrender
Into the competence of her hands.
Swath after swath I saw,
The flesh's apricot,
The spending hectic opulence
The blade left in her palm.

44

"I don't know all that much.
That's why I came."

                              "Why
Didn't you ask Eleanor?"

"I don't know. I didn't."

"Didn't you? She was the only one
Who knew about the 3.
How'd you find out?"

                        Tropical
Green and orange parings
Fell onto the dimestore-delft,
Cracked landscape of the plate;
Then, into the mortar-thick
Cream-colored bowl dropped
The mandorlas of the meat.

"I didn't. I was just . . ."

She laid the pressed flame
Of the seed among the parings
And stood, blade flourishing.
"Why don't you go home!"

"Well, I'd like to know why I'm here."

"Because you keep knocking after
You're locked out and you don't
Go away when you're asked."

"That's part of it. OK?
I'm not saying that's not
Part of it. What am I saying?"

The difficulty was
Not true and false. Nothing

Could be said to have been true.
The difficulty was
Dead reckoning with many rocks,
Waves breaking, and pitch dark.

"Irene, if I had known
About the number on the door,
I wouldn't have asked.
All right?"

"OK."

"I'm not
Trying to be difficult.
I like you, I don't know why.
I didn't even think
She was interested in women."

Mango has a resin in its flesh.
A ghost of the wood's flavor
Lingers at the root of the tongue.
Sizings of sap cover the teeth.
Each of us ate, taking
The bits of fruit between
A thumbtip and two fingers,
As though ritual could revive,
As though one could remember,
Or believe, what something meant.

"I don't know," she said. "We picked
Each other to be partners
Once in exercise class.
It just started happening."

"Yeah. You mean, Mondays."

I could feel myself held
At the ankles by the slender
Hands of Irene, pinned
In an exertion to sit up
For a twenty-eighth look
At the woman with a boy's grip
On my shanks, and the ceiling
Tilted while Irene's face,
Risen into view, spoke
Whispers of encouragement
That melted into the eddies
Of an old uneasiness below.

"I don't think we should feel
Guilty. Do you?" She was asking me.

"Why not?" I wanted to know,
But asking made her laugh.

"The only reason I could
Recognize you," she said, "was
I sneaked into her wallet one time.
She has this picture of you
With your hair all weird
And a comb under your upper lip
For fangs. That picture's it.
That's all I know about you.
She'd never tell me anything."

"That's an old Halloween present."

How could any of us three tell
Or ask another anything
But for an obvious,
Meanhearted reason?

The mango was gone by now
But for a golden ichor,
An alchemical tincture
Of the matrix of her eye,
Which I now drank, tipping
The mortar to my mouth,
Watching her watch me drink,
And when the runnel quit
My lips were on the rim.

"You want the other mango?"

"No, thanks."

       "Tea?"

          "No.
I think I'll wash my hands."

SEVEN

I washed with Dr. Bronner's
Peppermint Castile Soap,
The label of which taught,
In twelve hundred words
Of small, sans serif type,
Hygiene and Hillel's
Moral ABC:

    "1st: A human being must
    Teach 'Love His Enemy' . . ."
    Knowing the full-truth that unites
    All and not teaching all
    Is murder. Exceptions? None!

I washed, took a look
In the mirror, and looked
About the same. But my face
And hands were atingle, warm,
From the peppermint in the soap,
From the pepper part of the mint,
And, having closed both eyes,
I felt as though I were seeing
The rush of warmth in the lids,
Or as if that warm sensation
Were the seeing itself,
For Dr. Bronner was blinded
By an injury at Dachau,
Or Buchenwald, I forget.

Irene had begun to pace.

Facing the window bay
Across the vacancy of her room,
I straddled my chair backwards,
Chin on folded arms,

To watch the walk she brought off
Ostentatiously enough
En route, let alone
In the quartering of
A twenty-foot-square floor.

Or should I say she danced?

She went without plié
Or pirouette, without
An entrechat, alone
Without accompaniment,
Without pavane or polonaise—

OK, she walked—and how
She walked? She walked along
One wall, across the bay—
And toward and by and from
Her images in the windows
As though they could have been
Three coryphées—and back
Along the other wall
To veer mid-room there stop.

But—her hands—how
Should I say her hands went?

She was facing me now.
Feet still. Facing me. And her hands—
Did they go lightly? No.
In the heavy element through which
They rose, they would be lifted,
Glide into turbulence,
Maneuver, drop, and I
Would seem not to be there,
Would not seem, that is, and
Would begin to be there,

While she clenched her fists,
Heels of both hands forward
At her hips, feet wide-set,
Shoulders drawn back, back arched,
To reveal the ribcage with
Breasts pulled near to the bone,
And the musculature
Of the neck surmounted
By the overturned hull of the chin.

Low flame wandered over my features,
Faint and irreducible
As earthshine on an old moon.

And her body stood still facing me:
Feet shoulder-width apart,
Head tipped back out of sight,
Arms either side now
Rising, bending, joining
Overhead, and forming—
Wrist to wrist with elbows out—
A pentagon, the apex
Fisted   hinges   opening

Until her fingers stirred
Like cilia around an oral groove
To gather—from thin air
Into the space between
The elbows where no head was—
What? Whatever would be needful
To the motion of the legs:
A little moonlight, bulblight,
Emanations from the planets,
From red dwarves, from quasars,
Pulsars, from black holes.

She made calm exacting movements
And her head was tipped back
Out of sight!—legs flexed
At the knees, left footsole
Drawn in heel first on the line
Between right heel and crotch.

Where had her slippers and white socks gone?

Dance! To dance! But
Even though however
Yet still *dance*: limbs
On the ecliptic tilt toward solstice:
Spinning, dropping, motive
And unmoving dance! And
Irene danced!

    I wanted:
To be moved and was not—
Or was, not in the way
I'd wanted; for I watched
As though she could have been
Ardhanisvara (Shiva
In androgynous form)
Dancing the sublime destruction
By which torn seeds fall,
Or Shiva himself on the back
Of Ignorance, the pygmy,
Dancing till the spheres gaped,
And heretics could read
What gods, at the curtains
Of the riven firmament,
Read from spellbinding limbs,

As from her left foot, arch
Curved by the concentration
Of the calf—the free foot
Lifted into travel,

For the moment, like a dolphin
Between waves, between the former
And another ocean,
At the meridian, crossing
Into: an earlier hour;
A day with another name;
A differently numbered year:
Such was her left foot,
Lifted with toes pointing
To the plantedness of the right.

And I kept talking to myself
While Irene danced, not moving
My lips, talking, thinking
This cheap talk was what was wrong,
For Hindu deities
Had not much to do with
Eleanor's and Irene's affair—
To think of it! In this room!—
Or with a Knickerbocker dance
Which, as outlandish as it was,
Was no more farfetched than
My disparate turn of mind
Into contorted words:

If nothing is ever simple,
That is to say both that
Nothingness is forever simple,
And that no thing is, will
Be, or has been simple;
Nothing, hence, for the disparate,
Is, therefore, to the desperate,
Ever, in the dispirited
Turn of mind, then, *simple*,
If nothing is ever simple;
And so forth, to mince my words.

What syntax could describe
That body's authorship
Under an absence of her head?
Not mine. Nor could a whirling dervish
Have described my speechless
Sentences as they evaded
And collided with her namelessness.

She conquered my remove
With one foot imperturbable:
The right. The left. The right.
Arms overhead, no head, she came.

My throat twitched with slight
Strictures of oncoming speech;
My lips pursed; tongue crouched;
Thoughts would not be calm:
I was about to speak!

Not that I wanted to speak.
I wanted to know what
I was about to say,
Which meant to have said it—
Maybe, only to myself—
While I was hearing myself
Say, not to myself,
"Would it be all right if
I held you for a minute?"

And what of Eleanor? Irene
Remained in motion. I remained
Remaining to be changed:
Thoracic emptiness
With stammering detonations
At the core; abdominal
Corrosion; alum smack
Of mango in the throat;

St. Elmo's fire washing
The face and hands; welter
Of unreasonable thought.

One bare foot lifted
With arch forward planted
And one more. Again.
Again. Arrival without
Answer.

Question: "Irene?"

Head still tilted back
In occultation, arms
Around its absence, Irene
Came. I straddled my chair
Backwards, hands, like Buddha's now,
Palms up on separate knees.

She stopped between my feet.
Her pelvis nudged the back
Of the sleeping chair which moaned out
Of an inanimate sleep
While both her hands came down
To get their purchase on my face—
One thumb jamming my nose
Slightly to the left, the other
Poking my top lip into my teeth—
Hands tacky with gore
Of the mango, strangely warm,
As though I might be
Strangely cool, making me
Think Dr. Bronner's fire
Like foxfire lacked true warmth.

And Eleanor and I?

The fingers glided together,
Leaving me big chinks of light.
Was I supposed to be
Relieved to feel flesh touch
My flesh, extinguishing
The sight of my anxiety,
Or should I have been anxious
To prevent blindness? God

Damn her! No! What was the question
I should ask? Her fingers
Slid down to my temples,
And her face had come back
Mournfully inclined to
Complement mine. No!

My hands levitated with
Arms following their drift
Around her waist—the back
Of the chair between my chest
And her hip, thigh, belly,
And their conflux, while
Her tributary fingers
Pulled my head against her,
Cheek- to breast-bone, and
The image of her face
Remained.

Why must it remain
Mournful? Couldn't the lips
Have been drawn to the verge
Of smiling? Didn't the eyes
Look simply thoughtful?
Wasn't her forehead cloudy
From the strain of dancing?
No. The image of her face
Had one name: Eleanor's.

EIGHT

Irene switched the light.
She let the skirt fall
To her feet; peeled off
The leotard. The bellies
Of her breasts shone under
Boyishly small teats.

And I felt awkward — turning
To drape clothes on the chair
When she had let hers drop —
But, having turned away,
I could gauge what was up,
Rather, was not up — hung
With a fatuous air
Of brooding on deep consequences
No brain could have plumbed.

I turned back toward Irene.
The crux of her long stride
Was tufted in the dark.
Pale surfaces of her breasts
Looked cool, shone calm, came
Toward me, while I went
With an indecorous dangling.

Muscles in my arms and
Small bones in both hands ached
To have made the present
Seem to succeed the past:
One present, one past,
Forming a couple, strangers.

Irene: skin crotch-hair thigh
Breasts cushioning my ribs
Cheek on my shoulder
Breath spilled through fine hair

Along my neck my back
Cock caught between
Her groin and mine less
And now less flaccid

Eleanor! who preferred lights
Off, not one word during
Or about, whose lovemaking
I'd thought without variety.
It was! At home. Unless
Irene had been there. But
Irene: long and athletic.
Eleanor: the more
Voluptuous. Imagine!

We clung hard—muscle
Nerve blood bone
Exhorting us, "Now! Now this!"
To which the mind said, "Yes?"
And "Ah! Yes! This!" and "Then what?"

Fuck it! What did I care
Then what? What *now*? I
Pulled Irene down to me
Where, crouching, I lay back
On slats of lacquered oakwood.

She: "Wanna try the bed?"

I (lacking an erection):
"OK."

Why did she stop,
Left foot on bottom step,
Sidepieces in both hands,
Not climb, while I stood
Waiting, wondering
What lay between us

And the dark loft where
She looked? I made believe
Not to have seen them:

Seven steepling steps
Through spontaneity
Into the chosen world,
Up half a wooden stepladder
Secured with unbecomingly
Big nails.

I watched her climb.

No question of my choosing
Not to follow now
Under the sway of that dark
Flourishing between
The moons of her butt muscles,
None.

Now she was gone.

I found her lighting the candles
On all fours with dark tongues
Flickering at the tears
Of transformation which fell
Always into the two cusps
Of the candletops
To wash the bedclothes with
Shades of the flesh of mango,
Like the specular light
Thrown into a cave scooped
Empty at low tide at dawn.

But down there was empty,
Up here were the signs of life:
The television; magazines;
Books; bottles of red wine;

Wineglasses; waterbed;
Phone (which she was unplugging);
Philodendrons draped
On hooks and string over
The ceiling; stereo.

I fought not to be caught
Taking stock of her
Bookcase while she revolved
On all fours and I read
One name: le compte Donatien
Alphonse Francois Marquis
De Sade.

                Wait!

                        Anybody
Might have owned that book, been
Given it, no!—gotten it
As a joke. Don't jokes
Come out of nowhere sometimes?

        Physicists say, if,
        At the instant of the Big Bang,
        Things had existed, then,
        Their mutual attraction
        Would have had to be
        Too great to have been broken.
        Ergo: coming to be
        Was to be blown away.
        Ergo: the number zero.
        Ergo: the mango, green
        And ripe. Ergo: the mournful
        Splendor of each eye.

With room to stand up on my knees,
I stayed down on all fours
Observing catlike

Fluencies of her approach.
Our lips met in a circle
Of tongues on the threshold,
In a search to be searched,
Eyes—having had their try—shut,
Tongues rapt in their congenital
Yearning, and a mutual voice
Moaned in either throat.

Fallen onto my literal
Hands and knees petitioning,
Find me—I cannot,
I felt ridiculous.

It was ridiculous
To be alive, much less be here,
Firm in the nether head
Now, soft in the other,
And inside my ribcage
The continuous percussion
Blooming into love's extremity
While self-hate melted like
A tooth into the wound
And pain climbed into the tongue root
At its issue from the tastebuds
To be disembodied into
A smack of exultation.

I knew better than to laugh,
Except the monkey-fist
Of what's not funny but is
Laid into my breadbasket,
Latched onto my windpipe,
Jimmied open my jawbone,
And tore out a giggle.

She draw back staring.

Stared.

"Why do you laugh?" The uninflected
Tone of therapists
Whose manners come third-hand
Has irrepressible conviction
In your common-law wife's
Naked mistress who has just
Been tonguing your tongue
In the candlelight, and moaning,
Both of you, on all fours.

"I don't know why." If true,
Irrelevant. All right, "I
Thought we would look silly
If we saw ourselves now."
An invention, anodyne
Enough that, with slight
Strain about the eyes,
She hoisted the right corner
Of her mouth up, half
Into the semblance of a smile.

I rolled over the bedframe
Onto my back. The membrane
Of the waterbed shook
As the rippling hide on the flat
Breadth of a horse's neck
Does when horseflies light; then
Waves into which I sank;
And under them one heard
The joist-groan and the jamb-creak,
And I pictured my swift
Entrée into the downstairs
Salon through the ceiling
With a metric ton
Of water and a hard-on.

62

But the beams held while I rocked
And her wide shoulders pivoted
Step by step until
Her face above my face
Stayed at a scant remove.
The cross-rule of her smile
And perpendicular
Crease between eyebrows—brushed
By wingbeats of a summer
Tanagerlike light—formed
Characters of determination,

And I wondered, staring
Into that inverted look,
What energetic and
Illegible design
Was hers, and what was mine.

I tried to imagine
Eleanor's front teeth on Irene's
Clit making their pleasure
Strict enough with pain that
The release be double. Triple,
Considering my part:
Ignorant, made more so,
More to be instructed in
The paths of the marquis.

To imagine Eleanor!
Scrupulous, correct,
Intolerably good but
Expert to cause pain!
Improbable. However
There was what could change one
In the matrix of these eyes.
Or was that reflected?

They shut and her lips came open
And she drooped her head.
I tilted mine to join
In the inversion of
That kiss and of my life
Which followed.

NINE

What one felt, sunk
Into the cushioning
Water; what—with my skull
Pierced by her flexive tongue—
I felt: was: not just the usual
Doings (registries of sense,
Thoughts and critiques of thought,
Feelings, strugglings of conscience,
Memory, anticipation),
Although doings did, undid,
Did back, yet I could feel—
Or did I?—a not-doing too.

Is not-doing Being?
How can there be Being
When each hypothetical
Atomy of being is
Both x and y at once,
And x is (if and only
If) *not* y—energy
Not mass, velocity
Without location, particle
Not wave? When every tenable
Statement is deliberately
False, manipulated
By an unbeliever?
When mendacity, in the name
Of physics, is perfecting itself
Into an annihilation
Of itself through us?

For example: when the insulation
In a wiring room caught fire
From an open flame used
To detect air leakage,
The blaze spread for two reasons:

(1) The men responsible,
To spare themselves embarrassment,
Omitted to report the fire
Which (2) shortcircuited
Without setting off
The fire detectors.

Also
Incapacitated
Were the cooling systems
Due to the dysfunction of which
Meltdown became "unavoidable."

Dispelling rumors that
The "accident" involved
Bugs in the design, sabotage,
Political corruption,
Or a narcoleptic seizure
Of intelligent life on earth,
Investigations proved
The causes to have been "no more
Than typical 'human error'"
In the begetting of statistics:

80,000 people
Dead; 4,000,000 suffering
From contamination;
Maiming of the children
From these newborn on, past reckoning—

All of which may have not
Much to do with Irene,
Eleanor, or me, except
In a weird way of making
Every fact a variation
On the theme of error.

Dr. Bronner's fire was out.
The Marquis's fire was burning.

Irene crawled in bed with
Suckings at my neck and nipples,
Licks into my navel
Whither the tongue descending
Cupped onto my cocktip,
Trickled down the ventral
Vein with ticklings till
She took my left nut whole
Into her mouth and let
Teeth touch on the scrotum.

Eyes, in fear, came open —
Overhead to see her
Crotch licked by the two
Tongues of the candles
Lapping among philodendrons'
Valentine-shaped leaves.

Eleanor was no longer hot
To mouth my predilections,
Nor I hers. Ecstasy
In two years had subsided,
Was routine: twice weekly;
In the third year, less;
Now less. What? Once
Monthly? And while she'd had
Mondays to fall back on
I had comforted myself
With indignation. This
Was her fault. Everything
Could be her fault now.
Eleanor had done it.

                      Irene
Let the cutting edge
Be felt. I nipped the tendons
Between cunt and inner thigh;
Licked their hollows wet;

Blew, cooling; kissed; bit.
We'd begun by letting it
Be known: we both had teeth.
No harm in this. We had teeth
And would be of service.

Eleanor had more than
Done it though, she'd done it
With a woman. That was the clincher.
How could I be blamed
For being born a man?

I was exculpated then,
By gender, but there were problems,
Like my gender — which
Had opened into a nest
Of Chinese boxes: women
Within men inside women.

Head first, I had left the womb
To prove myself by self-
Annihilation; not
To permit mama's boy
To live; to be a man;
Never to cry; having cried,
Never to feel the reason.

Not that I came close to tears
In Irene's bed. I was delighted.
Strike that. I was delirious.

I'd let myself succumb.
I felt, reviving in the reviving
Pain of labor, a woman
Inside me, in my more-
Than-conscious mind, succumbing.
Hers was my surrender.
I was the still giving up

Of the woman I was
Within. Parturition
At my solar plexus
With an incorporeal rigor
Dragged on the latticework
Of muscle. In my body—
Inside, yet not of—
I felt, as of a vortex,
The deep opening *I am*:

My mutilated part
Transmogrified into
The principle of Love—as when
The lopped-off and dropped member
Of Uranus spawned, when Gaea
Had drawn the sickle, like a rib,
From her own bosom, and left
Kronos hacking himself out
From her obstructed womb.

Irene, adamant, bit
Hard, but not to sever;
Rolled my testicle
With slow, lubricious tongue
While I did lizard flickers
On her clit. One phoneme—
"Unh!"—ramrodded me
From her mouth.

Love!

What love?
Did I love Eleanor?
Hating her *was* torment.
That's indicative.
But could I love Irene?
I didn't even hate Irene.

An erection that taut—
That to be still hurt—
Meant something. If not love,
Something! Something profound.

Irene had quit the wandering
With her mouth to concentrate
On my mouth with her cunt,
Hips grinding, lumbar undulation,
My head rising, sinking
Under the driven bone,
Lips cushioning my teeth,
Slosh after slosh below.

What in the taste and smell
Of her made me feel strong?
Funky sourish mustiness.
Salt musk. Pungency veiled
In the mucous cloud that formed
Over the lesser lips.

Whatever it was got through.
I took her buttocks in both hands
And lifted her to see
The charge of quim slip
Into the channel between
Flushed swells of labia
Toward where I craned my neck
And tongue to kiss: her clitoris.

This was perverse, like anything
Superfluous to the brute,
Like knowledge, honor, shame,
But even the brute humped
In the candlelight
And moaned of its own accord.

I lifted her away
And craned up to the kiss,
A bodily intelligence's
Spiritual kiss,
Threefold, before an audience
Of three, one elsewhere,
Here by virtue—not by virtue—
In the agency of
Us both:

Our Eleanor,
God fucking all damn her
Straight to hell with her
Punctilious dumb show
Of indefinite rebuke
And guilt-founded sympathy.

Irene had all but come.
Her moans turned into whimpers,
And her whimpers had such
Fright-fraught regularity
As the complaint of
An abandoned pup.
The rhythm of her hip
Gyrations broke. Her shoulders
Came down on my hips,
Nails daggering my calves,
Teeth into my thigh while
I nosed at wet lips
And dilating muscle that
Gave in, came solid to
Clinch, clinch, clinch, "Ooonh!"
And her cry was, "Howw! Howaard!"

Was: my name—in stress
Reversed, and the reversal
Without meaning, as all names
Without meanings mean:

The name my father had
That he himself disliked
And gave, in spite of that,
To me; a name he had
Thought silly, but by which,
Through me, if only in pure
Silliness, he'd wanted to survive.

Howard, Jr., kissed Irene
More gently now, spreading
An effluence like all-heal
Over her tissues' spent
Ambition, and unrest.

Irene was heavy, pulled down by
What heaviness there was,
Unmoving, as though calm:
She cannot have been calm
With me, my blood full throttle
Cocked against her bosom,
While, mid-tendering of that kiss,
I laughed, in the remote
And broken recesses
Of thought, at Howard here,
Frustrated under a prone
Inverted woman's post-
Orgasmic drowse, as Eleanor
How many hundred nights?—
Had lain frustrated under him:
This, the woman, Irene,
Who'd been taking part, my part,
In Eleanor's and my love.

Irene shifted and broke off•
The kiss; turned, sending groundswells
Under me rebounding
From the frame; and lay alongside
My supine impassiveness,

Head ponderous on my shoulder,
Right hand lightly on my cock,
Leg hiked, hooked, over mine.

Eleanor, come home late
Monday, pecked my cheek
Hello. "These exercises
Relax everything."
She glanced (into my crotch?)
Sideways, touched her hair.

"Hm. You *look* nervous."

Bitch.
She made it clear that exercise,
Not I, was what she needed,
While she left obscure what
Exercise with whom.

"I'm not really the way
Eleanor thinks, am I?"

"No. She wouldn't say.
I mean, how should I know?"

That was the trouble, right?
Irene would not know; Eleanor
Not say; Howard not quit
Asking. What should they do?

Lie calm. Let Irene climb, come
Down spreadeagle, fluent
Into comprehending force.

"Yes! Yes!" I said, "Yes!"

No.

Is no yes merely—yes
To the unspoken?

"God, o, o."

Howard was in his o-phase,
Cock sunk full length into
Mild, miraculous Irene
Who, having come, came back,
Took him now, not from
Need of pleasure, but from
Faith in an idea,
In a theory of completion.

"O, o, o."

The little zero in Howard,
After the capital H,
After the goal-shaped itch,
The little o burst, burst
From an o-shape of his lips,
Describing the circular
Darkness of a dark
Encircling thought, the thought
Of the small o seizing
The pedestal of his cock.

"O." O Howard, Howard,
What will you do next?
When the hands that pin the shoulders,
The muscles stroking below,
The candlelit rondure of breast,
And inscrutable blue-gold eye,
Release, dilate, disappear,
Leaving Howard alone
In the New York City night.

"O." O Howard, what now?
Where? Where does one go?
Home. Where Eleanor is?
And tell. And tell her what?

"O." Howard, what kind of dreamer
Dreamt of fulfillment here
On uneasy waters tossing
Against the pinewood box?

"O." But what luck it was! Look!
Hands on the stirring hipbones
Of a specimen like Irene.

Not on the specimen,
Howard! On Irene herself.

TEN

Irene yet looked mournful,
Mournfully intent on
Any germ of pleasure
To be nurtured in the flesh,
As if it were unknown
Whose pleasure, hers or mine,
Might penetrate her next; yet
Both knew mine was now; yet
Hers seemed to have been growing.

And between the pubic bones
My fingers made slow becks
Into the sopping furrow,
Combed short, dampened curls;

And she took that hand then,
Cupped it to her breast, and
I cupped the other. Her
Hands let mine go and
Glided down her belly and
She leaned into my palms.
I craned again to kiss
Now blood-knotted nipples, and
Her fingers worked. She moaned
Low, largo, made slow bump-
And-grind.

              "O." I was there!
With gooseflesh, with constricted
Muscles, with electric
Charges leaping arclight, with
A wringing-out of organs,
And the thought of Irene
Sank into my spinal column,
Down the laddered backbone

Spilled, filled up my pelvic basin,
And my cry was, "I. . . ! I. . . !
Oooo!"

      To which hers was,
"Nnnn. . . !" The beginning, consonant,
And never-to-be-finished
"Now!" or "No!"

          Yet we
Were finished, done for, done with:
We, the two of us here,
Changelings; Eleanor too
Become a changeling. How
Though? How and which of us
By what imposture
(Other than recrimination)
Talk?—give the dumb due meaning,
Make terms for the long division,
Rend, and render into
Fragment, fraction, faction.

"Ohnh."

      By feigned mutual contentment?

Joist and jamb—which had
Been ticking (took two quick
Ticks, now three, none, rest,
Now tick overending
Into grunt and shudder
Of dead wood holding out
Yet in the deathgrip
Of laconic powers)—

Jamb and joist and water—
As if dumbstruck by
My would-be-manful
Essay at contentment—

77

Irene, jamb and joist,
And water, quieted by
Whatever causes, now
Seemed to be wanting to be
Sung to from the lovesong
Where that missed note of
Contentment keeps arriving
Off-pitch at the burden.

But my voice had failed me
Though my cock stood hard
As if to mock me with
A burlesque of conviction,
While a warm, slow-rolling
Drop of the mixed essences
Of Irene and Howard
Crossed an alert patch
Of my shaftskin onto a less
Alert patch of scrotum.

An erection that taut—
That to be still hurt—
Meant something. Not love,
Something.

When she sank, bone
Into bone, squeezed her vagina,
Squeezing drew up to
My crown's rim, and relaxing
Swooped in, throbbed against me
Three times, and lay quiet,
I could feel her movements
Pull the cloud inside me,
And I panicked.

Birth control!
Like I can afford half
Of an abortion now.
Carelessness is all.

                          Is
Not all maybe, not if
Pregnancy were part of her
Revenge on Eleanor for me—
Incidentally, on me too.

Don't be farfetched, Howard.
You don't even know the woman
To accuse her of a thing
Like that now.

                    Know her!
If I didn't know her,
How could she be pregnant
With my baby? I fucking know her
And I say . . .

                    Soft, her back was,
With concatenated
Muscle over ribbed vault
And smooth ass-dome, which
To follow with a careful
Hand was to have been transfixed
By the sequential shapeliness
Remembered in yet sounding
Music.

            And alive, to be
Alert, to be both
Disabused and more deluded;
In her arms held, to be
Holding, be betrayed,
Yet, at the piercing taste
Of the betrayal—be;
To feel the pangs with which
The muscles at the hinges
Of the jaw quake while the mouth
Fills with saliva. Be! Be

                    79

Here while barbed wire vibrates
In the solar plexus, melting,
Making the warm spot called

"Nnn. . ."

    "Ooo. . ."

                Grief, and in
Some instances, *hosannah.*

72280113